Pay Attention To Your Life

Pay Attention to Your Life

Reflections on self-awareness
and
self-determination

by

W. Marie Giles

Pay Attention To Your Life

Library of Congress Control Number: 2009910987

ISBN: 978-0-9728944-1-8

Cover design: W. Marie Giles
Book layout design: W. Marie Giles
Front cover photo: Heather Robertson

Printed in United States of America

Your life requires your attention. How you experience life is not based solely on your life, but on what you pay attention to during your life.

Acknowledgement

As I strive to constantly improve my relationship with God, I am grateful for His insights on the true purpose of my life.

I am grateful to my husband and sons for their support and understanding whenever I am inspired to get something down on paper — out of my mind and my heart — at some unusual time and place, with intentional haste, as the inspiration may vanish as quickly as it appears.

Foreword

It has been my experience to observe people constantly not paying attention to what they are doing, how they are speaking to others, where they are going in life, why they are here in the first place, and what their lives really mean.

I wonder if we realize how much we really don't pay attention—to ourselves or to each other. In this age of electronics and high technology, there are certainly enough distractions. Most of us use computers in some form or another in our daily lives. We have cell phones, personal digital assistants, portable music players, laptops or notebook computers, networked watches, and countless other devices that saturate us with infinite means of diverting our attention. We get news feeds, sports feeds, stock quotes, the weather, travel schedules, instant messages, and other "noises" that beg for our attention. How can we pay attention to it all and still take care of the main aspects of our lives?

Many accomplished motivational/inspirational authors have identified major dimensions of our lives to which we must attend in order to be successful and enjoy a meaningful existence. They may vary from author to author but, for the most part, they include these four areas: *mental, spiritual, physical,* and *emotional*. Paying attention to these basic areas, and making every effort to achieve some balance between them, could reap tremendous benefits for you and those for whom you care and with whom you associate. Indeed, if you are as physically fit as possible, you are able to accomplish those related tasks that would otherwise elude you. Likewise, if you are spiritually engaged, you tend to have an awareness of those things beyond normal comprehension. Emotional stability and health are as important as any of the others, as this allows you to deal with conflict and stress in ways that would become increasingly more difficult without it. And finally, mental acuity helps with the endless requirements for reading, writing, and planning.

These dimensions and their importance slowly became the basis for this book shortly after I derived the title. I was aware of the need to pay attention but did not want to treat such an important subject with too broad a scope. Therefore, I decided to examine how we could become more self-aware in the specific areas that we all share and, by doing so, begin to look at our own self-determination through attention to our lives in these specific dimensions.

As you read through the pages, digesting the words of wisdom, take some time to assess where you are in that regard. Allow yourself to become aware of your own habits and practices in these areas. Then make your own determination as to whether or not you could reap some benefit from adopting or following them.

If these words touch your heart and enlighten your mind in some small measure, then this book will have served its purpose. I welcome your feedback.

W. Marie Giles
mgileswb@att.net

Dedication

This book is dedicated to the memory of my dear mother who passed on in July 2001. I am truly blessed to have had her in my life. She taught me many life lessons that she probably never knew she had.

For Helen (Jeanne) - my dear sister, who passed on in December 2007: You were always such an inspiration to me and you always will be.

About the Author

W. Marie Giles is a wife and working mother of two boys. She has been on a journey of self-discovery and self-improvement nearly all her life. She has come to re-alize the journey does not end, for "it is in the journey that you continue to improve your outlook and reach a higher level of fulfillment." She also realizes the journey pauses at many destinations throughout our many phases of life. Paying attention allows her to be ready for each and every event along the way.

Marie's chosen profession is in the field of Infor-mation Technology where she currently works as a sen-ior manager in federal government service.

She resides in Pensacola, Florida, with her hus-band and their two sons.

Marie is also the author of "Open Your Mind, Open Your Heart: A collection of words of wisdom, heartfelt thoughts, and original poetry".

TABLE OF CONTENTS

Part I — Pay Attention To Your Life

Part II — Thoughts on Paying Attention

Part III — Attention-Provoking Poetry

Time is equal to life; therefore, waste your time and waste your life, or master your time and master your life.
— Alan Lakein

Part I:
Pay Attention To Your Life!

Attention

at·ten·tion (ə-tĕn'shən)

- Concentration of the mental powers upon an object; a close or careful observing or listening
- The ability or power to concentrate mentally
- Observant consideration; notice
- Consideration or courtesy

Pay Attention!

Chapter 1
Are We Really Paying Attention?

"The range of what we think and do is limited by what we fail to notice. And because we fail to notice that we fail to notice, there is little we can do to change; until we notice how failing to notice shapes our thoughts and deeds. " — R D Laing

Are we paying attention to our lives? I mean REALLY PAYING ATTENTION? Most of us never think much about what this means. We wake up, consider what we want to eat, take care of our personal hygiene, dress ourselves, and begin our **normal** activity for the day. At the end of the day, we go through a similar ritual, perhaps never really questioning why we are here in the first place. We just accept that we are here and go through a mostly mechanical existence. This is not living and it is not paying attention!

If there is one thing we can't afford to do, it's to NOT pay attention. Regardless of what we are doing, paying attention gives meaning to our lives and our lives require our attention. Our experiences in life are not based only on life itself. Rather they are based on the things we choose to pay attention to in our lives.

We must become intentionally aware and put forth conscious effort in order to get the most out of our lives, our environment, our careers, our family life, our health, and all of the things life has to offer.

If you fear your life lacks true meaning, joy, reflection, direction, or involvement, this book will share some insight into becoming self-aware and exploring a determination for your life's personal direction.

In the sections that follow, I present some thoughts which reflect on paying attention in the four basic areas of our lives: physical, mental, emotional, and spiritual. These thoughts are derived from my own personal research and experiences as well as key observations and significant experiences of others.

It is not the intent of this book to provide extensive information on the physical, emotional, spiritual, or mental dimensions of our lives. Rather it strives to offer some insight into the merits of simply paying attention to these four areas. It is my hope that it gets you noticing those areas where your attention is lacking and, conversely, those where, perhaps, there is too much attention with no return on investment.

Please
     Pay
         Close
             Attention...

A number of years ago, a newspaper reported a traffic accident. One of the drivers involved told a reporter, "There were plenty of onlookers, but no witnesses." Like life, huh? Plenty of people willing to observe, but few who truly pay attention to what's going on, and then bear witness, that is, get involved, act in some way on what they've seen or heard.
        — Anonymous

Chapter 2
Life's Four Dimensions

"The older I get, the more I realize the importance of exercising the various dimensions of my body, soul, mind, and heart. Taken together, these aspects give me a sense of wholeness. I want to be a whole human being ."   - Robert Fulghum

Try thinking of your life as having four major dimensions to which you must pay attention.   Balancing these dimensions are key to a more fulfilling life. Focusing more on one or two of these areas leaves you lacking in the others. In order to live the most meaningful, fulfilling life, you should make a conscious effort to give consideration to all four of these areas of your life:

__Mental__ — refers to the mind and its workings. Our mental dimension reflects how we think about our life, the beliefs we hold, as well as our conscious and subconscious thoughts. What we think in our minds determines largely what we will or have become, how we behave, and the way we set and achieve our goals in life. The mind is where we maintain a relationship with ourselves.

__Physical__ — pertains to the care and feeding of our body and includes our basic needs for nutrition, exercise, relaxation, and rest. This is our temple—the home we have been given to live in while on earth. It's not made to last forever. However, how we lead our lives depend, to an extent, on how we maintain our physical abode.

Emotional — reflects the heart of our being—the center of our emotions and feelings toward ourselves and others. This is where our attitudes are created or influenced. It is where our treatment of others originate. Love, anger, fear, happiness, and sadness are all examples of our emotions.

Spiritual — refers to the soul which is a non-physical entity capable of perception and self-awareness. The dictionary defines it as an attitude or principle that inspires, animates, or pervades thought, feeling, or action. The spirit is also referred to as the vital principle or animating force within living beings, mediating between body and soul. Although you can't touch it or even see it, we all feel our spirit within us.

Paying attention to these four vital areas of our lives promotes a balanced existence. When we neglect one area, the other three will suffer. Moreover, the consequences of neglecting additional areas are even more damaging. Each part is directly related to the others, which links the needs of one part to the needs of the whole person.

Given serious thought and attention, these four areas are really the composition of our lives. We must pay attention to them all.

"And thou shalt love the Lord thy God with all thy heart, and with all thy soul, and with all thy mind, and with all thy strength [body]: this is the first commandment." — Mark 12:30

Chapter 3
Pay Attention To Your Mind!

"To be conscious that we are perceiving or thinking is to be conscious of our own existence." — Aristotle

Paying attention to your mind involves knowing how you think and process information as your mind receives it. Whether the information is derived externally or internally is not as important as how you act on it.

The mind is the keeper of our thoughts. Our thoughts determine our actions. Constant knowledge of, and attention to this, help us govern our thoughts and plan our actions.

What you allow to enter and remain in your mind determines how you respond to the world around you. It can also affect your attitude, health, and other areas of your life.

Negative thoughts impact negatively and can result in misery and frustration. Positive thoughts allow positive interactions, better health, and a more willing attitude. When you maintain a positive attitude, through positive thoughts, you tend to see and find opportunities where others may not. You bounce back from failures or disappointment quicker than others who choose to brood over their predicament — which they arrived at by choosing a negative attitude. Our thought process and how we think are reflected in our attitude.

The Mind's Influence

The mind's influence on our actions cannot be un-derestimated. Thoughts are constantly entering our minds, mainly in response to any given situation. How we relate to the thoughts determines our response or re-action to the situation. Paying close and constant atten-tion to our thoughts can help broaden the space and time between when the thoughts occur and when we re-spond to them. The broader the space becomes, the more time we allow ourselves to think about our re-sponse and respond more appropriately. This is where we assess our options and make the choice that is best for the situation.

Becoming Mind-Aware

The mind can harbor all sorts of negative thoughts that we may not even be aware of. They may be in our subconscious, but our reactions to them are on the sur-face. Getting in touch with that part of the mind, or be-coming more mind-aware, raises our consciousness, not only to the thoughts but also our reactions, either direct-ly or indirectly, in response to them. If we focus on the fact that we always have a choice in how or when we re-spond to situations, we become more aware of the ability we have to change negative thoughts and actions into positive ones. According to Zig Ziglar, "Positive thinking will let you do everything better than negative thinking will."

Optimism or Pessimism?

You can choose to look at life either as an optimist or a pessimist – the "glass half-full or half-empty" adage.

Knowing that you have a choice becomes more evident once you begin to actively practice consciously choosing between the two. Focusing your mind on optimism and opulence, rather than negativity, is the very definition of a positive attitude. Your attitude controls the way you view everything around you and that which happens to you. Having a positive attitude will help you to respond to all things in a way that positively benefits you and those around you. A positive attitude benefits us with better health, less stress, more quality relationships, and happier feelings.

According to Aristotle, all human actions have one or more of these seven causes: chance, nature, compulsion, habit, reason, passion, or desire. We cannot change nature or chance – although you can sometimes improve your chances. We all have habits which we develop and which are often difficult, though not impossible, to change. We can change them if we are determined enough to do so. We can use our reasoning to do whatever we want to, although we sometimes act compulsively or without sound reasoning. We also often act on the advice of others based on our reasoning, desires, and passions.

The key point to all of this is: You are in control of your actions. You can choose how to react to your circumstances. No one but you can decide what your attitude is. Because you get to make that choice yourself, you have all the power. No matter what someone else does or says to you, no one can force you to have an attitude you don't want.

"What you plant and grow in your mind determines your destiny."

— Anonymous

"Your mind is like a tree, and the thoughts that enter your mind are like birds. It's not so important which birds light on a branch of your tree for a moment and then fly on. What matters is which birds you allow to build a NEST in your tree and make a home there."

— Unknown

Chapter 4
Pay Attention To Your Body!

"Every man is the builder of a temple called his body."
— Henry David Thoreau (1817-1862)

You only get one body. How you treat it determines how it services you. Paying careful and deliberate attention to your body's signals and symptoms helps you become a good steward of this responsibility.

Paying attention to your body involves being both proactive and responsive. There are some actions you can take to ensure your body is in the best condition without being prompted to do so. This is being proactive. On the other hand, your body is constantly telling you things you should respond to in order to ensure it remains in the best possible condition or to address issues related to certain signals and symptoms.

Proactive measures include the basics of eating healthy, regular physical activity, visiting the doctor and getting recommended screenings, and refraining from deliberately subjecting your body to inappropriate substances such as illegal or excessive drugs, smoking, overindulgence in alcohol, and any other harmful products.

Healthy eating. Developing healthy eating habits is a major step toward ensuring your body provides the services it was meant to. We know that our bodies require food for sustenance. We also know there are different types of food having different effects on our bodies. We've heard about the food groups and the food pyramid. We learned, at some point, which foods we should eat more and less of, how often we should eat, what we should avoid, and so many rules and restrictions that we often opt for convenience over trying to figure it all out. Our bodies suffer with regard to becoming overweight, under-weight, having low energy, illnesses such as diabetes, hypertension, heart conditions, and numerous other ailments, some of which we are not even aware of due to our failure to pay attention. We convince ourselves that some of the convenience foods we eat are healthy and good for us. What we really know is that, with the exception of some of the salads and fruit dishes, they are quick, convenient, and, for the most part, taste good, whether they are good for us or not!

Healthy foods, on the other hand, are sometimes avoided because they may take more time and effort to prepare, cost more, and are simply not convenient. What we should realize is that, despite some inconvenience, healthy eating is one of the things our bodies need to maintain good health. In this regard, we need to find ways to overcome these roadblocks and make the extra effort on behalf of our bodies. We should avoid trade-offs and pay closer attention to how the convenience foods are affecting our health and how we are treating our bodies. We need to become more educated and capable of determining and monitoring nutritional content such as fats, carbohydrates, and calories. Quick meals should not be the rule but rather the exception or occasional indulgence. Use caution when eating out. It is quite possible to eat healthy in restaurants when you have an idea of what the portions are and what they contain.

How do we change these long-standing habits of unhealthy eating? Determine what the roadblocks are, make every effort to overcome them, and choose to change the habits. We must become aware of how our bodies are affected and choose to protect them from these habits.

This is much easier said than done – believe me, I know it! However, our bodies will not last as long as they could it we don't consider changing. Below are some tips and resources to point you in the right direction. The rest is up to you. The tips require you to be attuned to your body and make a choice to cause a more positive impact.

<u>Tips for healthier eating</u>

- Don't wait until you are "starving" to eat.
- Try to eat 3 meals a day
- Eat more fruits and vegetables (if you can't or prefer not to go with fresh, canned is okay)
- Choose leaner cuts of meats
- Eat more fish and seafood
- Limit carbohydrates, especially after breakfast and particularly in the form of white breads, potatoes, pasta, and rice
- Limit snacking and choose fruit, protein drinks, and untoasted nuts
- Take your time while eating and realize when you have had enough
- Drink lots of water
- Don't eat when you are not hungry
- Limit caffeine and alcohol
- Don't smoke
- Pay attention to how certain foods affect your body. If there is an adverse reaction, avoid the

food and consult your doctor.
- Start small and build to a manageable level of change.

Resources for healthier eating

- www.healthierus.gov – a web site from the U. S. government containing all kinds of information on managing and improving your health.

- "A Closer Look at the Foods We Eat" Publication, http://dnrc.nih.gov/highlights/NutritionalFlyer-06.pdf

- Dietary Guidelines for Americans, 2005, http://www.health.gov/dietaryguidelines/dga2005/document/pdf/DGA2005.pdf - a publication that has been produced jointly every 5 years since 1980 by the Department of Health and Human Services (HHS) and the United States Department of Agriculture (USDA)

- MyPyramid.gov – web site from the Center for Nutrition Policy and Promotion, part of the USDA, established to improve the nutrition and well-being of Americans.

- ific.org – International Food Information Council Foundation web site is an educational segment of the IFIC. It provides science-based information on food safety and nutrition. The Publications link is particularly helpful.

- Nutrition.gov—provides easy access to food and nutrition information from across the federal government.

Regular Physical Activity/Exercise—Developing and maintaining a routine of regular physical activity is another important proactive part of paying attention to our bodies. By establishing this activity as a routine or habit, the chances of avoiding or abandoning it are diminished.

There are a number of benefits to regular physical activity. For one, it increases energy. It also increases stamina and endurance and allows us to feel more positive. Exercise and focused physical activity aids in weight loss.

When most people think of exercising it may conjure up a sense of dread, considering the effort that one perceives is involved. However, there are a number of methods from which to choose that could be interesting and fun. Some prefer running while others would rather walk. Still others utilize television exercise programs or video recordings to assist them in this endeavor. Yoga, Pilates, Tai Bo, kick-boxing, shadowing-boxing, T-TAPP, and numerous other methods are all available to address the many different tastes and temperaments. Try doing an internet search on some to these to learn more. Also, check the resources in the previous section on Healthy Eating.

Here are some tips to help you get started:

1. Start small and simple. Allow yourself to adjust to the idea of developing a routine of regular physical exercise.
2. Be creative. Move your arms and legs while sitting at your desk by tapping your hands and patting your feet. Take frequent breaks and

allow yourself to move around during that time. Walk a few extra steps around the building to enter using another entrance.

3. Join a fitness club and allow the staff to help you design a routine that works for you.

4. Try moving while watching television. Do some squats, leg lifts, push-ups, sit-ups, and anything else you can think of.

5. Don't push yourself too hard. Learn what works for you and how much you can tolerate. Build from there.

Your body deserves your attention. Don't let it down!

Doctor Visits and Scheduled Screenings— Scheduling regular doctor visits for routine check-ups or physical examinations, in accordance with a schedule recommended by your doctor, can go a long way in preventing illness or diseases before they become an issue. Depending on your history and condition, the doctor may recommend routine screenings or some other procedure to diagnose anything requiring attention. Without this, you risk allowing some condition to develop to a point beyond simple treatment or remedies.

Each office visit with a family-type physician usually includes blood pressure checks, weight and height measurements, reflex gauging, and checks for respiratory/breathing status. Many doctors order basic blood tests to determine if there are any conditions that warrant attention. Doctors rely on you to inform them of any symptoms you may be concerned about to help them make their diagnoses. Try to be open and honest to help them help you.

To determine what your individual schedule should be and what screenings you should be getting, start by consulting your family physician to advise you. Much depends on your medical history, current physical condition, age, ethnicity, and other factors. These are expert calls and well beyond the context of this book. Always check with your physician for advise concerning your health and well-being prior to beginning a new or different routine of eating or exercising.

Dietary Supplements— As defined by Congress in the Dietary Supplement Health and Education Act (DHSEA), which became law in 1994, a dietary supplement is a product (other than tobacco) that
- is intended to supplement the diet;
  contains one or more dietary ingredients (including vitamins, minerals, herbs or other botanicals, amino acids, and other substances) or their constituents;
- is intended to be taken by mouth as a pill, capsule, tablet, or liquid; and
- is labeled on the front panel as being a dietary supplement.

Dietary supplements may be used for a number of reasons. Some seek to compensate for diets, medical conditions, or eating habits that limit the intake of essential vitamins and nutrients. Others look to them to boost energy or to get a good night's sleep.

The Food and Drug Administration (FDA) suggests that you consult with a health care professional before using any dietary supplement. Many supplements contain ingredients that have strong biological effects, and such products may not be safe in all people.

If you choose to take a supplement, do so as safely as possible. Consider the following:

- Tell your doctor about any dietary supplements you use or plan to use
- Do not take a bigger dose than the label recommends
- Stop taking it if you have side effects
- Read trustworthy information about the supplement

"Or do you not know that your body is a temple of the Holy Spirit, who is in you, whom you have received from God? You are not your own; you were bought at a price. Therefore honor God with your body."

— 1 Corinthians 6:19-20

Chapter 5
Pay Attention To Your Heart!

"Keep thy heart with all diligence; for out of it are the issues of life. "   — Proverbs 4:23

The heart is reflected in the emotional dimension of our lives. It influences our personalities and how we feel about ourselves and interact with others. Physical likes and dislikes, sensual enjoyment, and aesthetic appreciation are all attributed to emotions. The overarching characteristic that links our hearts and emotions is feeling.

Many have spoken of the heart in terms of breaking, aching, loving, sadness, longing, full, empty, and numerous other emotions. The heart is a reflection of these feelings.

The emotional dimension governs our fears, desires, sadness, joy, and happiness as well as things like attraction and repulsion. This is also where we define our preferences, sometimes out of fear and anger. The state of the emotional heart is as important as keeping a physically healthy heart. It can affect mood, attitude, motivation, and confidence, among other states.

In order to pay attention to our emotions, we must first accept that we have a range of them. Once we do this, we must strive to understand them and their origins in order to help us control, change, eliminate, strengthen, or lessen them, as situations dictate. For instance, if you understand the source of a certain fear, you can try to find ways to face and conquer it.

One thing that can complicate emotional attention involves our failure to realize that we have repressed and not experienced or expressed certain emotions.

Emotions allow us a powerful means of communicating, giving us needed feedback about our life experiences. Once you are aware of these conditions that exist within the emotional construct, you can begin to pay closer attention and take some steps to monitor and address them.

The emotional state of the heart is linked to its physical state. Countless studies and observations have shown this to be true. When you pay close attention to your emotions and make the necessary adjustments, the heart will likely respond accordingly.

"A joyful heart makes a cheerful face, But when the heart is sad, the spirit is broken." Proverbs 15:13

"The best and most beautiful things in the world cannot be seen or even touched. They must be felt with the heart." — Helen Keller

Chapter 6
Pay Attention To Your Soul!

"Just as a mirror, which reflects all things, is set in its own container, so too the rational soul is placed in the fragile container of the body. In this way, the body is governed in its earthly life by the soul, and the soul contemplates heavenly things through faith."
— HILDEGARD OF BINDEN, letter to the Monk Guibert, 1175

Paying attention to your soul involves paying attention to your relationship with God. Nurturing the soul is as important as healthy nutrition, mental and physical exercise, and sleep. Developing a routine which focuses on the well-being of the soul will benefit you in similar ways as paying attention to the other three dimensions.

If you think of the soul as the foundation which holds the other dimensions together, you can see the importance of engaging in activities which will strengthen and sustain it. The most common way to do this is through spirituality.

Spirituality involves spending time praying, meditating, and reading or listening to tapes of the bible and other inspirational books. It also involves attending religious services and worshiping in formal and informal forums.

One of the best ways to practice your spirituality is to spend some time, on a regular basis, engaged in these activities. Reading the bible, meditating, reading devotionals or inspirational selections, and praying should usually be done in a quiet space where you are less likely to be interrupted. If you are seeking guidance, comfort, or a specific message, this quiet space will allow you to give your undivided attention to the voice you are expecting to hear. You may be seeking to understand your true purpose in life. You may be suffering from some illness or disappointment and need to be consoled. Having faith and believing in a higher power allows the practice of spirituality to bring results.

Many times we think our prayers are not answered. However, if we believe in God, we should always realize that His will is always what gets done. Getting in touch with your soul will help you discover your true purpose in life and show you the path you were meant to take. The message you have been seeking will be revealed to you as you become more aware of and provide the nurturing attention to your soul which is necessary to allow it to maintain and strengthen your connection with the Heavenly Father.

Take some time each day to experience some peace and calm, and engage in some form of meditation, prayer, devotion, or just listening for the state of your soul. As you progress, your soul will begin to speak to you and your life's purpose will emerge as the center of your being. You may be surprised to find you have already been living your purpose or that it may require a major change in your life. Either way, as you continue to pay attention, you will be enlightened.

Why do you hasten to remove anything which hurts your eye, while if something affects your soul you postpone the cure until next year?
— Horace

Part II:
Thoughts on
Paying Attention

∾⦿∾

Pay attention to the differences between you and others.

∾⦿∾

This refers to the differences between you and your mate, parents, children, siblings, superiors, subordinates, and others with whom you are in contact. They could represent strengths you need or wish to have or weaknesses you could help improve in yourself and others.

Try not to condemn the opinions of others simply because you don't share them. Everyone is entitled to their own opinion but not at the expense of trashing that of others.

Don't judge others who are different than you with regard to things like religion, color, physical characteristics, personality, or other traits. God made us all different but the same in the sense that we are all His children. If variety is the spice of life, these differences exist for that very reason.

᭯᭯ᐧ᭯᭯

Pay attention to how others perceive you.

᭯᭯ᐧ᭯᭯

If you pay attention to how others perceive you –
especially if you respect their judgment and opinion –
they may provide some insight into the real you. They are
letting you know, in some way, on some level – either ver-
bally or with body language – how your behavior and actions affect them. If you value them, this has even more
merit for you in paying attention to your life.

You may be giving off vibrations or energy levels of
which you are not aware and then wonder why you are
getting unexpected reactions. It may be because perception is sometimes stronger than the truth. The signals
you send are being received and acted upon in the manner in which they are perceived.

❦

Pay attention to your objectives.

❦

Make some choices based on long-term rather than instant gratification. Know what you want out of your life and make plans to achieve it. Don't settle for less than you deserve.

Set objectives and goals to become the person you perceive yourself to be and take action on those objectives. You won't be able to move forward on them unless you are paying attention to them on a regular basis.

෴

Pay attention to your possibilities.

෴

You don't know whether you can do something if you haven't tried. Step out and take a chance. Try something different in order to determine if you can, in fact, accomplish it. You have possibilities and they are limitless.

⚜

Pay attention to your potential.

⚜

You don't know whether you have the potential to do something if you don't reach for it. All of us can grow, get better, get wiser, and become so much more than who or what we are at the moment. Our potential to love, grow, forgive, give, and surrender the darker parts of ourselves is unlimited. The number of people we influence in the world can grow every day.

You won't ever know how far you can reach if you don't test your potential for stretching. Know your limits and don't be afraid to move beyond them.

You may have restrictions, disabilities, burdens, and conditions that hold you back, but in the essential areas of your heart, mind, body, and soul, you have unlimited potential.

"For our light and momentary troubles are achieving for us an eternal glory that far outweighs them all. So we fix our eyes not on what is seen, but on what is unseen. For what is seen is temporary, but what is unseen is eternal."

— 2 Corinthians 4:17-18

꧁ ꧂

Pay attention to your own uniqueness.

꧁ ꧂

Create your own thunder. Don't try to be something that you are not. God made each of us unique — no two exactly alike. You are your own individual — like no one else. Accept your uniqueness and find ways to make it work for you.

᪥

Pay attention to your actions.

᪥

Look before you leap. Avoid doing something you will regret by thinking things through before acting. Impulsivity can be a deal-breaker — either in the form of words or actions. Become aware of how your actions impact others in your relationships, your work, and your life.

∽✫∾

Pay attention to your words.

∽✫∾

Think before you speak. Choose to correct kids rather than constantly criticizing them. Choose loving and kind words for your spouse. Give encouragement to friends and family rather than seeking to discourage their likes, dislikes, interests, or practices.

If you would not want it said or done to you, don't say or do it to anyone else.

"As you wish that men would do to you, do so to them."
— Luke 6:31

༼ༀ༽

Pay attention to your curiosity.

༼ༀ༽

Ask. Answers do not exist without questions.
If you want to know about something or someone,
don't be afraid to ask. If the situation calls for discre-
tion, recognize that. If you can obtain the answer in
another manner, be curious enough and seek other
ways to find it, such as research through reading
books or other publications and searching the internet.

Don't ignore your curiosity. It can help you become more knowledgeable, informed, and aware of
what is going on. Some things that may prompt your
curiosity include:

- A desire to know or learn.
- A desire to know about people or things
- An object that arouses interest
- Something novel, odd, or different

Curiosity is an important part of life. Through a
desire to learn or know, life continues to promote itself and keep itself alive. A lack of curiosity can lead
to a lack of a fulfilled life.

❦

Pay attention to your practices.

❦

Don't just advocate it – live it! It may sound cliché to say "Practice what you preach." However, this is good advice to those who tend to say one thing and then actually do something completely opposite. Someone is always watching your behavior and practices. Don't do anything you would not want to appear in tomorrow's newspaper, on a social network, or revealed in a meeting or other gathering.

Another thing to consider is putting into practice the things you learn. When you acquire a skill, knowledge, or abilities, put them into practice to get better and reap the benefits that were your original intention. Otherwise, don't waste time learning things you have no intention of using or putting into practice.

⚜️

Pay attention to your personal journey.

⚜️

You're never really there – the journey is continuous.

As long as forces abound to test your resolve in any area of your life, you are subject to setbacks. But, don't discourage or despair. The important thing is to continue the journey. Enjoy your accomplishments, but don't expect anything to last forever. The fact that you have strength and the will to continue ensures that you will get back up sooner each time. "Happiness is a journey – not a destination."

෴

Pay attention to your own prejudices.

෴

Be aware of opinions you form that are not based on fact. When you pre-judge a thing, situation, or person, you may end up having to re-think a decision or opinion or even apologizing. If this is a common practice, pay attention to how often the other side of the story changes your original opinion. If it is not a common practice with you, still pay attention so you avoid it and prevent it from becoming so.

"We are each burdened with prejudice; against the poor or the rich, the smart or the slow, the gaunt or the obese. It is natural to develop prejudices. It is noble to rise above them." — Author Unknown

"If you judge people you have no time to love them."
— Mother Teresa

❦

Pay attention to how you spend your time.

❦

Do you think constantly about things you want to accomplish yet convince yourself there is not enough time? Perhaps you are not paying enough attention to how you are using your time. When your objectives are important enough, you will find the time to accomplish or achieve them.

If you think a particular objective requires a large amount of time you don't have, try breaking it into smaller tasks and complete them over time.

Are you wasting your time on things that add no or little value to what you want to accomplish in your life? Spending endless hours watching television, with no return on the time invested, limits how much you can accomplish otherwise.

Become more aware of how you spend the time you are being granted each day. Ask yourself if you are furthering your chances of fulfilling a dream, living your purpose in life, or making a valuable, lasting contribution to other than yourself. The answers may surprise you.

Pay attention to your attitude.

Many say attitude is everything. Whether you believe it or not, it is worth considering. Do you pay attention to your attitude during the course of a day? A week? A month? Is it mostly negative or positive? Either way, think of where it's getting you in your life. Is a negative attitude hindering you or is your positive attitude helping you to see the "half-full" glass? Read one of my poems, below, and know that you can choose to be negative or positive. Either way, if you pay attention, you'll notice a difference.

Optimism/Pessimism

Optimism is its own reward.
It's much like when we draw a lucky card.
It helps us realize our hopes and dreams,
And the task-at-hand is easier than it seems.

Pessimism seeks to bring us down,
And makes our face a constant, gloomy frown.
It strips us of our hopes and dreams,
And takes away our drive and self-esteem.

Just realize the choice is yours to make.
Be careful that it's not a big mistake.
For one will make your life a living hell.
The other will keep you happy and living well.

Which do you choose?

∽⊙∣⊙∾

Pay attention to your motivation.

∽⊙∣⊙∾

What gets you motivated? What keeps you motivated? It's important to know what motivates you to act — or not — in various ways at various times. Determine whether it's good or bad sources and if it's internal or external.

If you maintain an awareness of what motivates you and whether it is coming from a base that is good or bad, you are in a better position to control your actions, thoughts, and the consequences or benefits of such motivation.

⌒⊙⌒

Pay attention to your appearance.

⌒⊙⌒

Your appearance has a lot to do with how people perceive and treat you. In relationships, job interviews, at work, in and outside of the home, and just about wherever you go, appearance is considered. Others pay attention to whether your hair is well-groomed, how appropriately you dress, your personal and dental hygiene, and many other aspects of your appearance. Since others pay attention, why shouldn't you?

What is your appearance saying about you? What type of image are you trying to convey? Does your appearance represent you the way you want and deserve to be represented?

The bottom line is: your appearance says a lot about you. Think about the impression you want to make. Others view your appearance as representative and reflective of who and what you are as a person. Right or wrong, fair or unfair, this is reality.

☙❦❧

Pay attention to your habits.

☙❦❧

A habit is defined as an acquired pattern of behavior that often occurs automatically. These behaviors represent a dominant or regular disposition or tendency or a prevailing character or quality. Habits are acquired behavior patterns regularly followed until they become almost involuntary

Many common habits like smoking, nail-biting, substance abuse, overeating, personal mannerisms, gambling, and regularly interrupting may adversely affect those around you, including family, co-workers, and friends, without your even paying attention to it. Other habits, such as regular exercise, healthy eating, focusing on the positive, which can be considered good ones, should also be noticed relative to how they impact you and others.

Are you aware of your many habits — good and bad — and how they may be impacting your life? As Aristotle put it, "We are what we repeatedly do." Are your habits serving you or are they limiting you or reducing your effectiveness in your life? Think about it.

ᖍᘐᕱ

Pay attention to your body language.

ᖍᘐᕱ

Your body language represents signals that you give in your interactions with others. This includes things like eye contact, facial expressions, gestures, posture, body movements, and tone of voice. Some of these signals provide important, non-verbal information without speaking a word. Non-verbal behaviors make up a large percentage of your daily interpersonal communication.

By paying closer attention to your non-verbal behaviors, you can determine what signals you may be giving unintentionally. You can also choose how to better communicate in this manner. Becoming more conscious of these signals will help you use your body language to your advantage and not have those signals misinterpreted, misread, or used against you.

You can develop this behavior by paying careful attention to these body signals, how others are responding or reacting to you, and practicing different types of non-verbal communication with others. By noticing non-verbal behavior and practicing your own skills, you can dramatically improve your communication abilities.

⊷⧓⊶

Pay attention to your routines.

⊷⧓⊶

Routines are commonplace tasks, chores, or duties that are done regularly or at specified intervals. They are typical or everyday activity that are more or less unvarying and are also referred to as a customary or regular course of procedure.

We develop routines to ensure we get those things done which require regular attention. This may include things like paying monthly bills, cooking dinner, submitting weekly or periodic reports to supervisors, regular meetings, annual doctor visits, vacationing, and many other repetitive, planned tasks.

Sometimes, routines can limit our growth as we become locked into a particular way of doing certain things or a certain time to do them. This keeps us from considering other options to improve the way we do these things.

What routines do you follow? Are they meaningful? Do they add value to your life? Are they limiting you from exploring other possibilities? Give this some serious thought and see if there may be a need to change, add, or eliminate some routines you have practiced over time.

Part III:
Attention-Provoking Poetry

On the following pages are selections from my collection of original poetry. Most of these poems were inspired by some event, person, or feeling I experienced and was compelled to express it in writing.

Although these poems may not all be directly related to the four dimensions or the thoughts on paying attention in the preceding sections, I hope you enjoy reading through or relating to them, or just being amused or inspired by them.

I hope they provoke your attention.

Good and Bad Times

When times are bad, look to the sky;
Then you can hold your head up high;
And know that things will work out right,
Never out of mind, never out of sight.

When times are good, bow down your head,
Each night before you go to bed.
Give thanks to God for all He's done
And how He takes care of His own.

I Am

I am who I am
No matter what you say.
You can look at my face
Or you can look away.

I know who I am
No matter what you think.
Like a chip that floats
Or sandbags that sink.

My One And Only Love

I think of you as roses red,
And sweet as fragrant dew,
That falls upon the earth at dawn,
And calls me close to you.

You are my one and only love,
To you I pledge my life.
My faith and honor are yours to keep,
For you my darling wife.

My Knight in Shining Armor

You are my knight in shining armor
Ever ready when I call.
You've been with me through good and bad times,
Sickness, good health, and all.

And through the years we've grown together
Rich experiences beyond measure.
I wouldn't trade our life and time
For any material treasure.

To you, my knight, I pledge my heart
Along with all my love.
Our destiny, our fate intertwined
A union blessed from above.

My Mother, My Rose

A Mother's love is like a rose
whose scent lingers with her offspring,
reminding them of her petal-soft heart,
protective thorns,
and long-lasting beauty.

Will I Be Missed?

Will I be missed when I am gone?
Will anyone cry for me;
For all the things that I have done
And all I tried to be?

Will they soon forget my name
And then dismiss the time
That I existed on this earth
And the deeds I left behind?

Or will they sing – rejoice for me
'Cause I tried to live a life
That helped to ease this ailing world
Of a little stress and strife?

Sometimes I wonder if I've done
What I came here to do.
And when I pray and ask the Lord,
He lets me know what's true.

For all that I have done and seen
It matters still, you see,
That I have made a lasting mark
And many will weep for me.

Life

We think we have it all figured out.
We think we know what life is all about.

Thinking that we know just what to do
"Live and Learn" but is that really true?

For some this is easy
And life is good.
For others nothing seems to turn out
As it should.

Some are living life from day-to-day
Others seem to constantly go astray.

Still many others tend mainly to look ahead
While others simply wish that they were dead.

Such is life...

Depression

Do you ever get so depressed
You cannot do a thing?
You try and try to shake it
But it's almost like a dream.

You try to wake yourself up
With good and positive thoughts
But your mind and body won't react
The way you think they ought.

You'll have to wait until it passes
And returns control to you.
So reconcile yourself to that
And soon a light shines through.

Many times it's over
Not long after it starts.
Other times it lasts so long
It tears into your heart.

Try to maintain hopeful thoughts
To send it on its way --
Knowing you will wake up soon
Ready to face another day!

Another Chapter

As you complete this chapter in life's book
Take some time to have another look

At all the ones that you have put behind
And think about just how they did unwind.

Sit back, relax – recall the happy times;
Never erase those memories from your mind.

Do not forget the times when things were sad;
Lest you forget there's always good and bad.

You may have had some hard times in the past;
But there's no reason why they have to last.

No one said it's easy growing up;
Survivors, by their nature, must be tough.

Well you have shown the world that you can make it.
Whatever life is giving, you can take it.

The book of life is many chapters long,
Filled with stories of the weak and strong.

The time is now to choose the one you'll be;
Have faith and hope – it all works out –
You'll see!

God's Will

If there was any other way
Your dear one would still be here
To comfort you and care for you
And calm all of your fears.

But God has put a will in place
Neither you nor I can change.
He also makes us strong enough
To suffer through hurt and pain.

Remember all the times you've shared
And let that comfort you.
Think of what your loved-one would
Have wanted you to do.

It may seem now the time you had
Was too short to comprehend.
You wonder why it had to be
Such a quick and sudden end.

But keep your trust and faith in God
And know that He is near.
Just like your loved-one's spirit
Which you will always hold dear.

Tender Moments

A mother's heart holds lots of Tender
Moments which she gives
To those for whom she loves and cares
Each and every day she lives.

A father's strong and tough demeanor
Won't readily reveal
The Tender Moments within his heart
That he safely conceals.

A child brings us Tender Moments
When born into the world.
They give us a measure of hope and joy
Whether it's a boy or a girl

Tender Moments can be revealed
In efforts to save a life.
They're evident in words spoken
Between a husband and wife.

Tender Moments are what we need
With them we can't go wrong.
They get us through the bad times
And keep the good times strong.

Tender Moments are what we make
When we show others we care;
Reaching out and comforting,
Opening our hearts to share.

Tender Moments warm our hearts
And help us through our days.
Whether they are given or received
They work in wondrous ways.

So share a Tender Moment
With a loved-one or a friend.
And let them know how much you care
Over and over again.

Prayer for Sons

Dear Lord, hold him in your hands
And let him make good choices.
Keep him safe from hurt and harm
While hearing the heavenly voices.

Let his will be strongly set
Where he will do his best;
Always ready, always prepared
For any trial or test.

Let the good within his heart
Shine through any mask.
And may he know that you are there
With him through every task.

Make Your Own Garden

You must make our own garden
However it grows;
What it will produce
Only God knows.

Until the sun rises,
And blooms start to appear,
Keep tending your garden,
Year after year.

Each day, give it love
And nurture it, too.
Its fruit will bring bounties
And rewards just for you.

Keep tending your garden
And it will do well.
How strong it becomes,
Only you can tell.

Always remember,
That which you give,
Comes back many times,
For as long as you live.

A garden that's beautiful --
Full of life and good deeds --
Is what you must strive for
When planting your seeds.

Keep Dancing

Dancing is living
And life is a dance.
With each step you take,
You're taking a chance.

The music you hear
Is what helps you keep moving --
Fast or slow,
Hopping or just grooving.

As long as you listen,
The rhythm won't stop.
Whatever the beat,
It keeps you on top.

The world is your stage
For the performances you'll give.
Make each one a better one
For as long as you live.

Seeing Yourself As Others Do

Seeing yourself differently than others do
Can limit your success.
'Cause others see the good and bad,
Which you might not assess.

To see their views, look inside,
Where all your secrets rest.
Be honest with yourself and them.
Put yourself to the test.

Seeing yourself as others do
May change your point of view,
Your attitude, your outlook,
The things you say and do.

The **way** you say and hear things
May also change, it's true.
And how you view the world, at large,
May seem to be brand new.

Don't hesitate, don't be afraid
To take this chance to know,
How this small step can change your life
And the direction you choose to go.

Once you have come to terms
With who you really are,
The rest will fall right into place
And your life will be richer, by far.

Find The Courage To Find Your Voice

If you have something "real" to say
That others may want to hear,
Find a way to cast aside
Your reluctance and your fear.

You'll never know how well you'll do
Until you've given it a try.
Don't sit inside your man-made shell
Until the day you die.

What you'll say could change a life,
Or bring a bright, big smile.
It could even mend a broken heart,
Or touch the soul of a child.

So get prepared, take the chance,
And let your heart be your guide.
Open your mouth – the words will flow,
You'll be really glad you tried.

True Meaning

Dear Lord, help us to understand
The true meaning of it all;
As we proceed throughout our lives
When we rise and when we fall.

Help us know that you are there,
Whether things are good or rough.
Fill our minds with ways to "make it",
Whenever life gets tough.

Lord, touch our hearts and let us know,
Through the sunshine and the rain,
The true meaning of a particular thing
Is that it is never, ever in vain.

What Matters Most

A physical body, worn or torn,
Matters less and less you see;
Than an open mind and a caring heart
And who we were born to be.

Each and every one of us
Was placed here for a reason.
We must continue to seek and search
For our own individual season.

What matters, then, the most dear friend,
Is that we realize,
That our true purpose in this life
Is filled with sacrifice.

We may not always get the things
We pray for from above.
What matters most is that our God
Has ways to show His love.

He gives us life with special meaning
When we're willing to pay attention.
He keeps on nudging us with hope
Despite our own dissension.

Sooner or later we start to see
Just what his messages mean,
If we have faith and stand steadfast
Believing in things not yet seen.

Just The Two Of Us

When it was just the two of us,
We did a lot together.
It didn't matter – hot or cold -
Or whatever the weather.

We'd walk along a crowded street,
Holding each other's hands;
Oblivious to passers-by
No worries, no demands.

We'd laugh and joke and jump for joy,
Whenever we came near
The place where we would always know
There was nothing to fear.

For in the arms of the one you love
Is comfort – safe and warm.
And feelings of a life and love
Free from hurt and harm.

Hope and Faith

Having hope is important,
Because we know that the Lord
Will preserve our faith and fortitude
As long as we do our part.

We must reach out to others
Giving them kindness and thought
And continue to maintain hope
That God will not leave us distraught.

In the face of disaster and devastation,
When things look hopeless and grim,
We wonder and cry "Why us 'O Lord!"
But we continue to have faith in Him.

Hope is a critical part of faith –
Praying and wishing without knowing.
If faith is believing in things not yet seen
Then hope is what keeps us going.

We were granted the ability to hope
So our faith could remain without waver.
Even when we don't get what we hoped for,
Our faith keeps us strong and in His favor.

When We First Met

When we first met
You knocked me off my feet!
The last 30 years have been
Even more of a treat.

We've shared the good
Sometimes the bad
And Oh My Love
What a time we've had.

Raising kids
And working hard
We put our trust
And faith in our Dear Lord.

This day is so very special
To share with you my love
An angel sent directly
To me from Heaven above.

In another 30 years
I pray that we will be
Still living this beautiful dream
I for you and you for me.

Always and forever
Leaving each other never.

The Years

The years have gone by
So fast it seems
While we were so busy
Fulfilling our dreams.

Raising kids
And busy with careers –
We barely took time
To count the years.

Now here we are
At number 27 –
Still loving and living
A page from Heaven.

The next round of years
Will bring joy and hope,
Though we must contend
With whatever the slope.

The love we've shared –
Year after year –
Will keep us moving forward
Without reservations or fear.

Missing You

There's a little hole in my heart,
Growing bigger every day.
It's there because I'm missing you
Since you went away.

I try so hard to fill my days
To help set aside the pain.
But no matter how hard I try
It just seems to be in vain.

Don't let this hole keep growing
Without stopping in to say,
"Hello, Mom, I miss you too."
That will surely make my day!

It's Your Life

Your <u>body</u> is a temple
Given by God to you.
Treat it with the utmost respect
And your ailments will be few.

Your <u>mind</u> should not be wasted
On useless, idle fare.
You may awaken one morning,
And find it's no longer there.

Nurture a clear, clean <u>spirit</u>
And seek to be close to God.
As long as you keep this in mind,
From Him you will never, ever part.

Temper your heated <u>emotions</u>
For God has given to you
The power of careful, thoughtful response
In everything you do.

Attention to these four dimensions,
When practiced day-by-day,
Will help you lead your very best life
In every possible way.

A Letter From Heaven

I was given a little time
Down there on God's green earth
He set the time for me to leave
Even before my birth.

He's giving you a little more time
So you can let others know
The Lord has all our plans in His hands
It's true, He told me so.

He controls the sun and moon,
The stars and all the rain.
And sometimes He will put us there
With lots and lots of pain.

Not because He doesn't care
Our teachings tell us that.
His sacrifice was the greatest of all
No one can argue the fact.

I know you do not understand
How God could let this be.
I knew the moment He called my name
He had a better place for me.

The pain and all the suffering
In my human form are gone.
But, Mom, I just need you to know
I'll never leave you alone.

I will visit with you from time-to-time
Throughout every single day
You may see and feel me there
Although not in a physical way.

Just look around and witness
God's miracles, great and small
I just may be there in the midst
A helper at His call.

I'll always love you, Dearest Mom,
And cherish our times forever.
Until we meet again, in Heaven,
My Spirit will leave you never.

It's Never Too Late

It's never too late to live your life
The way you think you can.
It's never too late to let the world
See that you have a plan.

Start using all the lessons
You've learned year after year.
It's never too late to stand up and shout
"Hey, world, know that I'm here!"

Once you can accept your life
For its true purpose – whatever the call --
You'll see the world take notice
And you'll forever be standing tall.

The most important thing to know --
As you decide to proceed --
Your life is just what you make it.
Believe this and you'll succeed.

Sometimes it takes more courage
Than you ever believed you had.
Sometimes you have to "just do it"
And say, "That was not so bad!"

Now why not try to find out
What's really holding you back?
And once you do you'll notice
It's nothing that you lack.

For all you need to move forward,
Has already been given to you.
Just know that the choice is yours
And that will get you through.

It's never too late to play this game
No matter what others say.
And no matter the discouragement,
There's no better time than today.

Helping Others

When you reach out to others,
And help them in their plight,
You become a better person
In dealing with your own personal fight.

They really will appreciate
The tireless things you do,
In getting them back on a track
That eases their pain, too.

So never stop your giving
And helping others strive
To get their lives together
And continue to feel alive.

No matter what you do or say,
It's still the only way.
So reach out to another,
And fulfill your purpose today.

<u>Sadness</u>

There's a sadness that sometimes surrounds me,
I can't seem to control.
I try real hard to reject it,
But it seems to take its toll.

I try to think of more positive things
To make my heart feel good.
But that doesn't always help me
As much as I think it should.

Lower and lower I seem to sink,
Engulfed by doom and dread.
What is this thing that comes over me?
What must I do instead?

Prayer is the one sure thing
That helps the hurt or pain;
And asking for a ray of hope
To get me through the rain.

Soon, before I know it
He shines His light on me
I release my burden unto Him
And I know he will set me free.

The Hole Grows Bigger

The hole in my heart got bigger
When the next son went away.
I didn't think I could miss him
So very much each day.

Sometimes I sit and think of them
And how it used to be
When they were home and still around
Just Dad, the boys, and me.

These feelings of great loneliness --
Each day they come and go.
Sometimes I'm up, sometimes I'm down
And still I miss them so.

Finding things to do for me
And catching up on life,
Helps to keep me focused and
Relieves a bit of strife.

No matter how far away they are
And no matter what they say
The hole in my heart will continue to grow
A little bit more each day.

An Old Soul

An old soul has left us
And taken her place with God
We will sorely miss her.
But our memories will not depart.

She inspired us to live our lives
Without malice or regret --
Always showing us that, with her,
What you see is what you get.

We always embraced her candor,
Her humor and her grit;
And so many times she charmed us
With her knowledge, wisdom, and wit.

The inspiration she gave to us
Will live on in times to come.
This lets us know, deep in our hearts,
She was truly a chosen one.

"Good-bye" is not the phrase to use;
"See you later" is a better one.
For our faith tells us we'll see her again
Whenever our earthly time is done.

(For Dierdre)

Are you paying attention?

Self-awareness

Awareness of oneself as an individual

Aware of oneself, including one's traits, feelings, and behaviors.

Self-determination

The act or power of making up one's own mind about what to think or do, without outside influence or compulsion.

The process of defining one's own direction

After Word

Thank you for your interest in this book. I hope you enjoyed reading it and were able to gain some insight into to your own personal quest to pay closer attention to your life as you move toward your destiny.

When I began writing this book, after I had decided on the title, I had not yet heard of Eckhart Tolle's book, *"A New Earth: Awakening To Your Life's Purpose"*. During some downtime from my writing, I decided to read it and participate in Oprah's worldwide internet broadcast class featuring the book and its author.

As I watched the broadcast, I so identified with the method of which he spoke to allow you to awaken to life. It runs parallel with paying attention to your life. I felt secure in the fact that my book is in sync with these teachings and revelations. The more we pay attention the better equipped we are to awaken to our true purpose in life.

If you want to pursue this journey further, I highly recommend reading the works of Eckhart Tolle, particularly, *"A New Earth"*.

W. Marie Giles
www.hihenterprises.com
mgileswb@att.net

Additional Resources

The following books and tapes have contributed to my journey and may prove useful to you in your journey of self-discovery.

Stephen R. Covey
- The Seven Habits of Highly Effective People
- First Things First (with A. Roger Merrill and Rebecca R. Merrill)
- Living the 7 Habits
- Principle-Centered Leadership
- The 8th Habit

Don Miguel Ruiz
- The Four Agreements
- The Four Agreements Companion Book
- The Mastery of Love

Colin Creel
- Navigating Your Calling and Career

William P. Young
- The Shack

Gary Zukav
- The Seat of the Soul
- Soul Stories
- The Heart of the Soul

Dr. Viktor E. Frankl
- Man's Search for Meaning

John C. Maxwell
- Make Today Count
- Today Matters
- The Maxwell Daily Reader

Sarah Ban Breathnach
- Simple Abundance
- Simple Abundance Companion
- Something More
- A Man's Journey to Simple Abundance

Carol Adrienne
- The Purpose of Your Life

Les Brown
- Live Your Dreams

T.D. Jakes
- Maximize the Moment

Denis Waitley
- The Psychology of Winning

Brian Tracy
- The Psychology of Achievement

Gary R. Collins
- You Can Make a Difference

Dr. Mark Thurston and Christopher Fazel
- The Edgar Cayce Handbook for Creating Your Future

Todd Hopkins and Ray Hilbert
- The Janitor: How an Unexpected Friendship Transformed a CEO and His Company

Sean Covey
- Seven Habits of Highly Effective Teens

James M. Kouzes and Barry Z. Posner
- The Leadership Challenge

Cheryl Richardson
- Take Time for Your Life
- Life Makeovers

Florence Littauer
- It Takes So Little to Be Above Average
- Your Personality Tree

Dr. John M. Oldham and Lois B. Morris
- The New Personality Self-Portrait—Why You Think, Work, Love, and Act the Way You Do

James Redfield
- The Celestine Prophecy
- The Tenth Insight
- The Celestine Prophecy: An Experiential Guide

Eckhart Tolle
- A New Earth: Awakening To Your Life's Purpose

Malcolm Gladwell
- Blink
- The Tipping Point

Dr. Phil McGraw
- Life Strategies
- Getting Real
- Self Matters

David Allen
- Getting Things Done

Joel Osteen
- Your Best Life Now
- Become A Better You
- It's Your Time: Activate Your Faith, Achieve Your Dreams, and Increase in God's Favor

Guideposts
- Daily Guideposts: A spirit-lifting /devotional

Philip Yancy and Brenda Quinn
- Meet the Bible: A panaroma of God's word in 366 daily readings and reflections

Gay Hendricks
- Five Wishes: How answering one question can make your dreams come true

Brenda Pace and Carol McGlothlin
- The One Year Yellow Ribbon Devotional

Eckert Tolle
- A New Earth
- The Power of Now

Rhonda Byrne
- The Secret

Barack Obama
- The Audacity of Hope
- Dreams From My Father

ORDER FORM

Heart-in-Hands Enterprises
P.O. Box 3757
Pensacola, FL 32516-3757

Pay Attention to Your Life
Reflections on self-awareness and self-determination

Please send me ___ copies of **Pay Attention to Your Life** at $16.99 per copy. Add $3.00 for shipping and handling. Make check or money order payable to **Willie M. Giles**.

Ensure Check/Money Order Enclosed

Please send the book(s) I have requested to:

_____
Name (Please print)

_____
Address

_____
City   State   Zip

ORDER FORM

Heart-in-Hands Enterprises
P.O. Box 3757
Pensacola, FL 32516-3757

Open Your Mind, Open Your Heart
A collection of words of wisdom, heartfelt thoughts, and original poetry

Please send me ___ copies of **Open Your Mind, Open Your Heart** at $12.00 per copy. Add $3.00 for shipping and handling. Make check or money order payable to **Willie M. Giles**.

Ensure Check/Money Order Enclosed

Please send the book(s) I have requested to:

_____
Name (Please print)

_____
Address

_____
City   State   Zip

www.ingramcontent.com/pod-product-compliance
Lightning Source LLC
Chambersburg PA
CBHW072202090426
42740CB00012B/2353